My State

NEBRASKA

By Christina Earley

TABLE OF CONTENTS

A Crabtree Seedlings Book

Crabtree Publishing
crabtreebooks.com

School-to-Home Support for Caregivers and Teachers

This book helps children grow by letting them practice reading. Here are a few guiding questions to help the reader build his or her comprehension skills. Possible answers appear in red.

Before Reading:

- What do I know about Nebraska?
    - *I know that Nebraska is a state.*
    - *I know that Nebraska grows a lot of corn.*

- What do I want to learn about Nebraska?
    - *I want to learn which famous people were born in Nebraska.*
    - *I want to learn what the state flag looks like.*

During Reading:

- What have I learned so far?
    - *I have learned that Lincoln is the state capital of Nebraska.*
    - *I have learned that every year volunteers plant 30,000 plants at the Sunken Gardens.*

- I wonder why...
    - *I wonder why the state flower is the goldenrod.*
    - *I wonder why there is a mammoth skeleton at the University of Nebraska State Museum.*

After Reading:

- What did I learn about Nebraska?
    - *I have learned that Chimney Rock is 325 feet (99 m) tall.*
    - *I have learned that the state animal is the white-tailed deer.*

- Read the book again and look for the glossary words.
    - *I see the word **capital** on page 6, and the word **volunteers** on page 14. The other glossary words are found on pages 22 and 23.*

NEBRASKA
Hi! My name is Ezra.
Welcome to Nebraska!

I live in Lincoln. There are many **historic** buildings in Haymarket Square.

The largest **mammoth** skeleton is in Lincoln at the University of Nebraska State Museum.

Nebraska is in the **midwestern** United States. The **capital** is Lincoln.

Fun Fact: Omaha is the largest city in Nebraska.

The state animal is the white-tailed deer.

The goldenrod is the state flower.

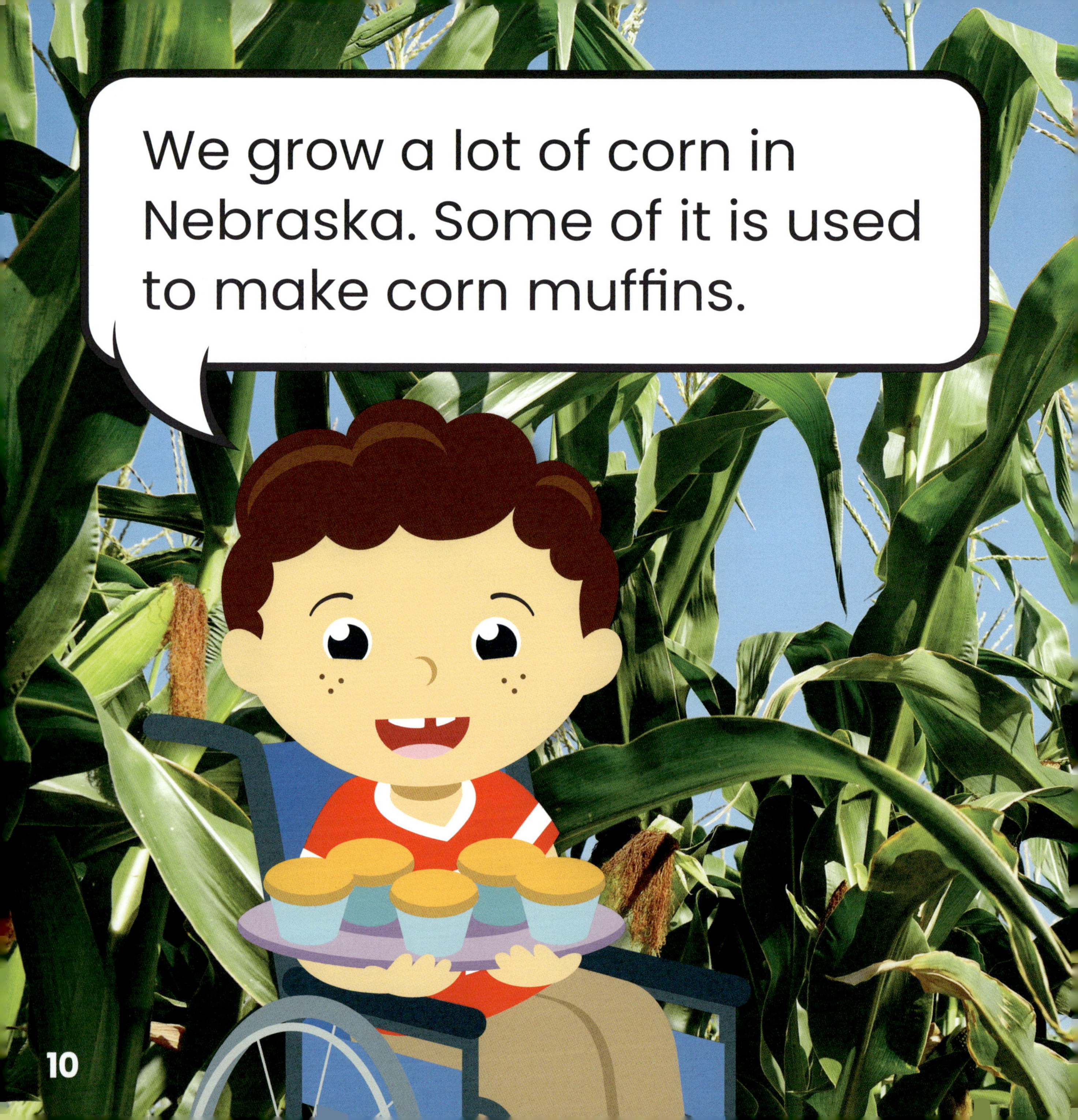
We grow a lot of corn in Nebraska. Some of it is used to make corn muffins.

Fun Fact: Nebraska is one of the states that grows the most corn in the U.S.

My state flag is blue. The state **seal** is in the middle.

The Nebraska Cornhuskers football team has won five national championships.

I like to visit the Sunken Gardens. The flowers and statues are so pretty.

Fun Fact: **Volunteers** plant 30,000 plants each year.

I like to visit Chimney Rock National Historic Site. Chimney Rock is 325 feet (99 m) tall!

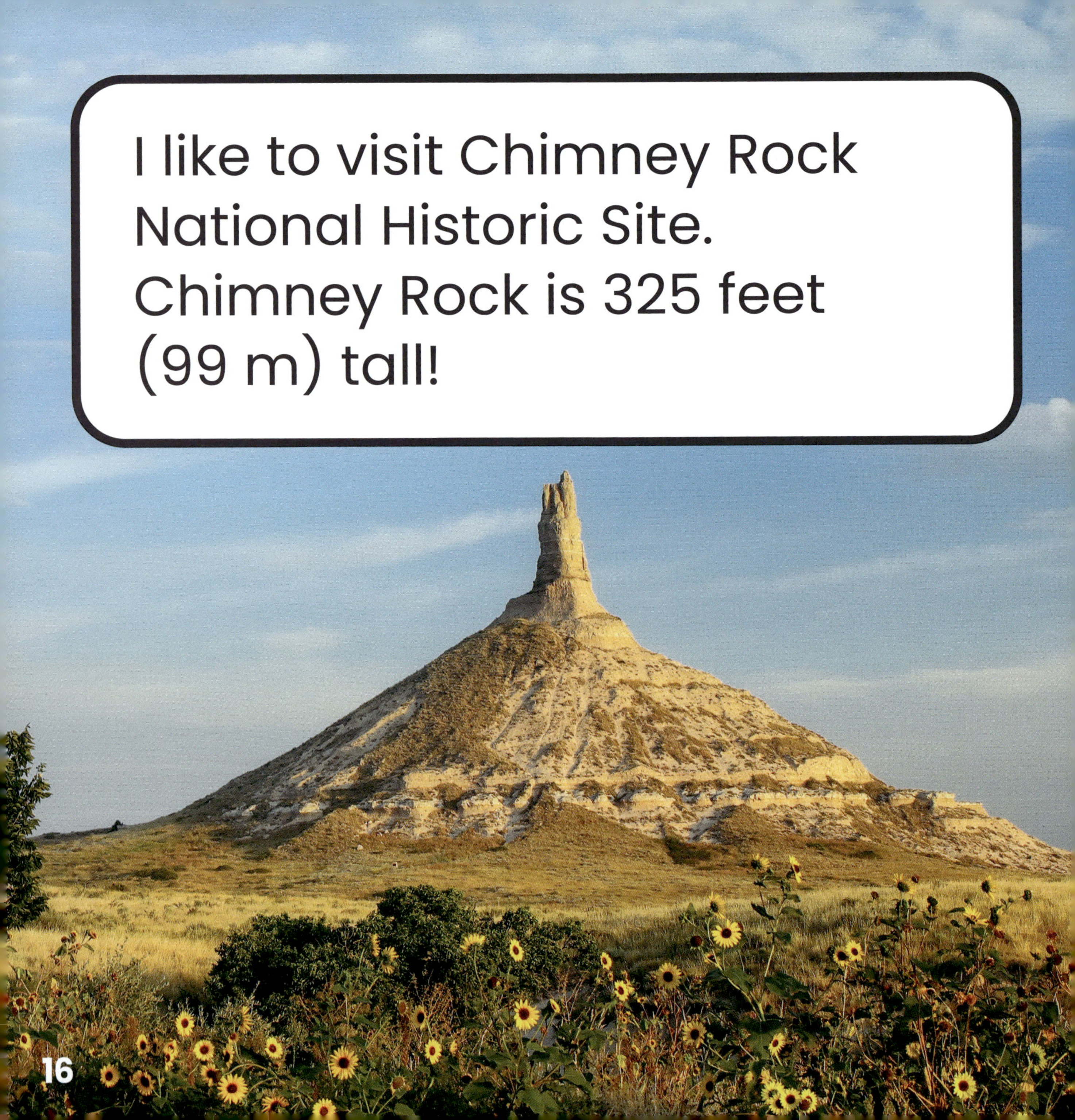

My family and I learn about what life was like at a military fort in the 1800s at Fort Atkinson.

Dancer and singer JoJo Siwa was born in Nebraska. Baseball player Wade Boggs was also born in Nebraska.

Fun Fact: President Gerald R. Ford was born in Omaha, Nebraska.

I like to visit Omaha's Henry Doorly Zoo and Aquarium. The blue monkeys are my favorite animal.

I enjoy fishing in the North Platte River.

Glossary

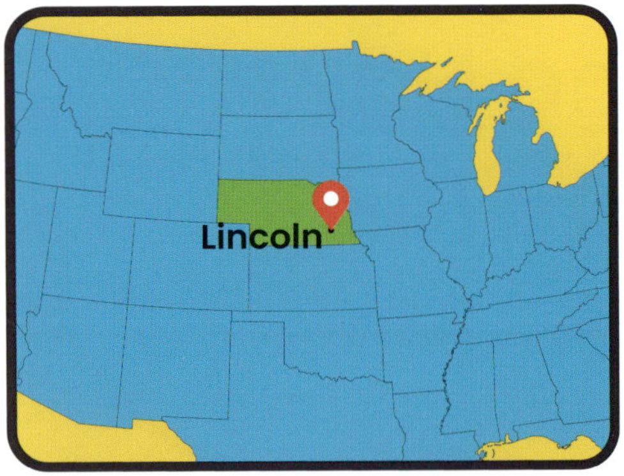

capital (cap-ih-tuhl): The city or town where the government of a country, state, or province is located

historic (hi-stor-ik): Something that is important in history

mammoth (mam-uth): A type of large, hairy elephant from a long time ago

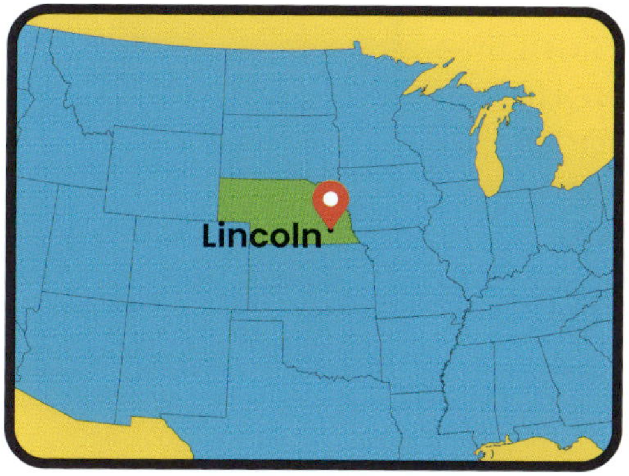

midwestern (mid-west-urn): The northern central part of the United States

seal (seel): A special design that is used on important papers and other items

volunteer (vol-uhn-teer): A person who willingly does a job without getting paid for it

Index

About the Author

Christina Earley lives in sunny South Florida with her husband and son. She enjoys traveling around the United States and learning about different historical places. Her hobbies include hiking, yoga, and baking.

Written by: Christina Earley
Designed and Illustrated by: Bobbie Houser
Series Development: James Earley
Proofreader: Melissa Boyce
Educational Consultant: Marie Lemke M.Ed.

Photographs:
Alamy: Ian Dagnall: p. 4, 22; PhotoStock-Israel: p. 5, 22; Roman Numeral Photographs: p. 18 right
Newscom: Nick Tre. Smith/Icon Sportswire DHR: p. 13
Shutterstock: Don Mammoser: cover; Shutterstock: p. 3; Volina: p. 6, 22-23; Aspects and Angles: p. 7; Tom Reichner: p. 8; Yulia_B: p. 9; Serg64: p. 10-11; Fotokostic: p. 11; railway fx: p. 12, 23; bmr3n3: p. 14, 23; Jenn1030: p. 14-15; Don Mammoser: p. 16; Ruth McNeill Photography: p. 17; Tinseltown: p. 18 left; evantravels: p. 20; Joseph Sohm: p. 21
whitehouse.gov: p. 19

Crabtree Publishing

crabtreebooks.com 800-387-7650

Printed in the U.S.A./072023/CG20230214

Published in Canada
Crabtree Publishing
616 Welland Avenue
St. Catharines, Ontario
L2M 5V6

Published in the United States
Crabtree Publishing
347 Fifth Avenue
Suite 1402-145
New York, New York, 10016

Library and Archives Canada Cataloguing in Publication
Available at Library and Archives Canada

Library of Congress Cataloging-in-Publication Data
Available at the Library of Congress

Hardcover: 978-1-0398-0524-8
Paperback: 978-1-0398-0556-9
Ebook (pdf): 978-1-0398-0620-7
Epub: 978-1-0398-0588-0